WHEN SPOONS ARE LOW

ALANA SEJDIC, Ed.D.

ORIGINAL ART BY
BLANCA FLOR

For Z

Yes, I'm tired.
Yes, I'm slow.
Yes, I know I said I'd go.

I'm hurt,
I'm worn,
I took a tumble.
Right now I feel I might crumble.

Sometimes I struggle
and need assistance.
I am always thankful,
despite some resistance.
You say you won't judge me,
then you look at me with pity.
What I want is for you
to preserve my dignity.

Wait, slow down
don't do it for me.
I need support,
and my autonomy.

I am capable,
powerful and strong.
Don't call me "special,"
that's just wrong.
No, I'm not special,
I'm just me.
And I'm fine as is,
so leave me be.

I need help like anyone,
but here's something you must know:
I am self-determined.
If you don't get that,
then you should go.

Raise me up,
don't hold me back or push me forward.
I can steer my own ship,
you can come aboard.

Show me love,
but please don't smother
be a friend
a teacher,
sibling,
mother...

Give me a hand when spoons are low.
When they are back in stock,
you'll know.
Together we can be community
not just all of you...
then me.

This world is full of worthless "isms."
We need to stop and recognize
we all deserve, we all belong.
No matter
color, shape, or size.

Ability?
Yes, I have it.
Disability?
I have that too.
But what shall we say of you?

An ally?
Yes.
A support?
That's true.
A friend?
That's good.
I love you too.